ENCOURAGEMENT FROM SCRIPTURE:

A Help for Those of Us Who Have Days When We Can't Even Get Out of the Car Without Praying First

By Diana K. Mitchell

I0539862

Jones Bush & Ward Publishing Co., Inc.

Concord, North Carolina

Encouragement From Scripture: A Help for Those of Us Who Have Days When We Can't Even Get Out of the Car Without Praying First
Copyright © 2024 by Diana Kay Mitchell

Scriptures reference the King James Version of the Bible.

Because of the dynamic nature of the Internet, any Web addresses or links contained in this book may have changed since publication and may no longer be valid.

The views expressed in this work are solely those of the author and do not necessarily reflect the views of the publisher, and the publisher hereby disclaims any responsibility for them.

Library of Congress Control Number: 2024951534

ISBN: 979-8-218-55591-7 (pbk)
ISBN: 979-8-218-55592-4 (ebook)

Table of Contents

We are entering a place in time where we, as Christians, will begin to say, "truth need not be validated any further," but we will also have a knowing within us that during this time we must continue to proclaim The Truth for those yet to be saved.

In the name of Jesus, the living GOD, I dedicate this book to those who will continue to contend for the faith once delivered to us all.
Remember who GOD is.

Message from the Author

Hello. Thank you for purchasing my book. To get the most out of it, please stop and read the scriptures that I have associated with each of the 30 sayings (the main texts) that I've written. These sayings derive from scripture, were written at the prompting of Holy Spirit, or have been drawn from sermons (2) that I heard preached once. I started working on this project after I got an idea for a t-shirt for Pastor Appreciation Day. I was still perfecting that t-shirt design, and other designs, when Pastor Appreciation Day, October 31, 2024, came and went. My Pastor Appreciation Day t-shirt then became a "You are appreciated!" t-shirt as I continued to develop the text for other t-shirts that became the main texts of this book.

During development, to keep track of everything, I placed my t-shirt designs in a folder titled "Encouragement From Scripture." When it came time for me to decide on the title of this book, it dawned on me that everything in that folder had indeed encouraged me whenever I felt like giving up to continue with my life, and with the Christian faith. Hence the title and subtitle, "Encouragement From Scripture: A Help for Those of Us Who Have Days When We Can't Even Get Out of the Car Without Praying First."

From that perspective, it's worth noting that we would have no true knowledge of GOD were it not for seminarians, theologians, preachers, deacons, teachers, musicians, and evangelists—all pastors (shepherds/ministers) of the word of GOD. Because of what I've learned throughout my years, I want to encourage you to **continue** in your life, and in the Christian faith, with JESUS. I've been where some of you all are now in that there are days when you can't even get out of the car without praying first. I want to assure you that what GOD has given us through the Bible is more precious than gold, more durable than rubies, and as certain as death, so don't be afraid, and don't give up. Instead, as Jude encourages us, contend for the faith.

Make studying scripture, and prayer **daily habits**. Ask GOD questions concerning the texts in the Bible, and be on the look-out for GOD's reply. As you continue to do this, and draw closer to GOD as a result, I promise you, those days where you can't even get out of your car without praying to GOD first will significantly decrease (even though the situations causing them remain). I know that they did for me.

It should be noted that one page in this book is dedicated to the Psalms. They are special to us because they speak of the coming of Christ, and they teach us that it's good to express our joy, happiness, gratitude, and love to, and for, GOD. They also teach us how to constructively express our anger, fear, sadness, and pain to GOD in way that acknowledges our negative emotions without allowing those emotions to consume us. In other words, the Psalms teach us how to pray. Psalms that express anger, fear, sadness, and pain generally talk through those emotions and then end with hope. The exception to that is Psalm 88, which acknowledges that sometimes we really can't see hope. During those times we need and want GOD to see and understand both the depths of our despair, and our hope for GOD's rescue. When those times come, remember Psalm 23. We walk **through**, with GOD, difficult situations in our lives: Because of the finished work of CHRIST JESUS, we do not set up camp and live in perpetual dismay. Sometimes it's an unconscious or deliberate stroll, sometimes a slow and stumbling walk, but we do get through the valley of the shadow of death.

I pray in the name of the living GOD CHRIST JESUS that GOD open your eyes and bless you to see your unseen help. You are not alone.

Sincerely,
Diana Kay Mitchell
diana.mitchell@dianakmitchell.com
December 25, 2024

How to Read this Book

The main text in this book has been placed on the right-hand-side (recto) pages. The left-hand-side (verso) pages have been, for the most part, left blank for note-taking by the reader. The main recto pages are divided into two boxes separated by a bookmarker graphic (yes, that orange/yellowish graphic on the page was supposed to be a hand-drawn, well-worn, gold-colored bookmarker). The smaller box on the left side of the bookmarker contains **scriptural references** for the text in the larger box on the right. Readers should read the content of the larger box before reading the content in the smaller box. The larger box is divided into three parts: the first line of text, the **page header**, tells the reader what the page in its entirety is all about, and it is used as the **Table of Contents (TOC) header**; the large text beneath that, the **main text**, is the key take-away text of the page; and, the line of text beneath that contains a **one-line reminder** that, it is hoped, acts to re-enforce all of the text on the page. Some pages also contain text boxes visually scattered throughout the main text area in order to give the reader **additional information** in regard to the main text. Each TOC header consists of three recto pages with the exception of the final 12 TOC headers (**Belief** through **The Truth**). Those TOC headers consist of one recto page each. After the TOC header, the main text should be read followed by any additional information on the page, followed by the one-line reminder, and finally the scriptural references. Please don't forego taking the time to actually read the scriptural references in the Bible. As a unit, they, in my opinion, make the page do what it's supposed to do: help you understand the biblical text.

In order to gain a full understanding of the main text, the scriptural references, which follow the order of the Bible, should be read top to bottom. Scriptures for the second **Testimony** (Evidence), the last **Trust in GOD** (the Psalms), and **The Truth** recto pages have been grouped for the reader in the hope that reading them in the suggested order will help to further clarify the main text. Each scriptural reference section refers the reader to 12 books in the Bible. Testimony, Trust in GOD and The Truth TOC headers are exceptions. Two of the recto pages for the Testimony group contain references to 10 books in the Bible, the third references only two books in the Bible. Two of the Trust in GOD recto pages reference 12 books in the Bible, the last one (the Psalms page) refers the reader to only the book of Psalms. As a counterbalance, The Truth recto page references 11 books in the Bible.

The only other exception regarding the recto pages is the **Knowledge of GOD** page. The scriptural references are in order, but they are grouped by text color. The gray text highlights Saul's failure to perform his first task: wait seven (7) days. The red text highlights the differences between Abraham, Saul, David, and JESUS regarding their individual relationships with GOD. Abraham spoke with GOD, and therefore was known by GOD. No scripture was recorded concerning Saul's personal relationship with GOD, and in the end, with his lack of knowledge of GOD, GOD became "thy god" to him. Contrast this against David, who announced GOD as "the living God." And JESUS, himself GOD, used scripture. Saul, however, is not alone. Even today, many of us ignore the Exodus "I will" directive from GOD, and place our own strength ahead of GOD's—utterly destroying people in the process instead of utterly destroying the altars of false gods along with their idols that can neither see nor hear nor save.

For those who are not Christian: In this work, chapters within a book of the Bible are divided by using a semi-colon (;) between chapters; verses within a chapter are divided by using a comma (,) between verses; and, text to be read from one verse to another verse, as with a section of text, are notated with a dash (-) between the verse numbers. When a section starts in one chapter and ends in a different chapter, for clarity, the author has placed a space before and after the dash. A colon (:) mark indicates the chapter number of a book on the left side of the colon, and the verse number(s) on the right side of it. When there is no colon, then the number references the entire chapter, excepting the five, one-chapter books in the Bible (Obadiah, Philemon, 2 John, 3 John, and Jude). Numbers for those books simply reference verses.

Accountability

EVERY KNEE WILL BOW, EVERY TONGUE WILL CONFESS: JESUS IS LORD

Genesis 1:1-3;
49:8-12
Numbers 24:1-9,
17, 19
2 Samuel 12:1-25
Ezra 5:1-17; 6:1-2;
6:3-15
Psalms 35:23;
72:1-15;
95:1-6;
104; 150
Isaiah 45:22-23;
55:5
Ezekiel 8
Daniel 5:30-31;
7:13-14,
27
John 1:1-5; 13:13;
20:28
Romans 9:5;
10:9;
14:8-11
Philippians 2:9-11
Revelation 5:11-14

MY LORD AND MY GOD.
THE ONE BALAAM SAW,
JESUS,
SEES ALL, KNOWS ALL.
MATTHEW 4:1
MARK 1:12
LUKE 4:1
JOHN 1:1-5

Every knee; every tongue. Ps 145:10-13; 1 Cor 15:45-47

7

Notes

Joshua 24:14-15
1 Samuel 16:7
1 Kings 3:5-14
Psalms 20; 23;
        118:8
Isaiah 31:1-3
Jeremiah 17:5-8
Micah 7:7-8
Matthew 6:24-33
John 14:5-6; 15:5
Acts 4:12; 19:13-20
1 Corinthians 10:13
Hebrews 11; 12:1-3

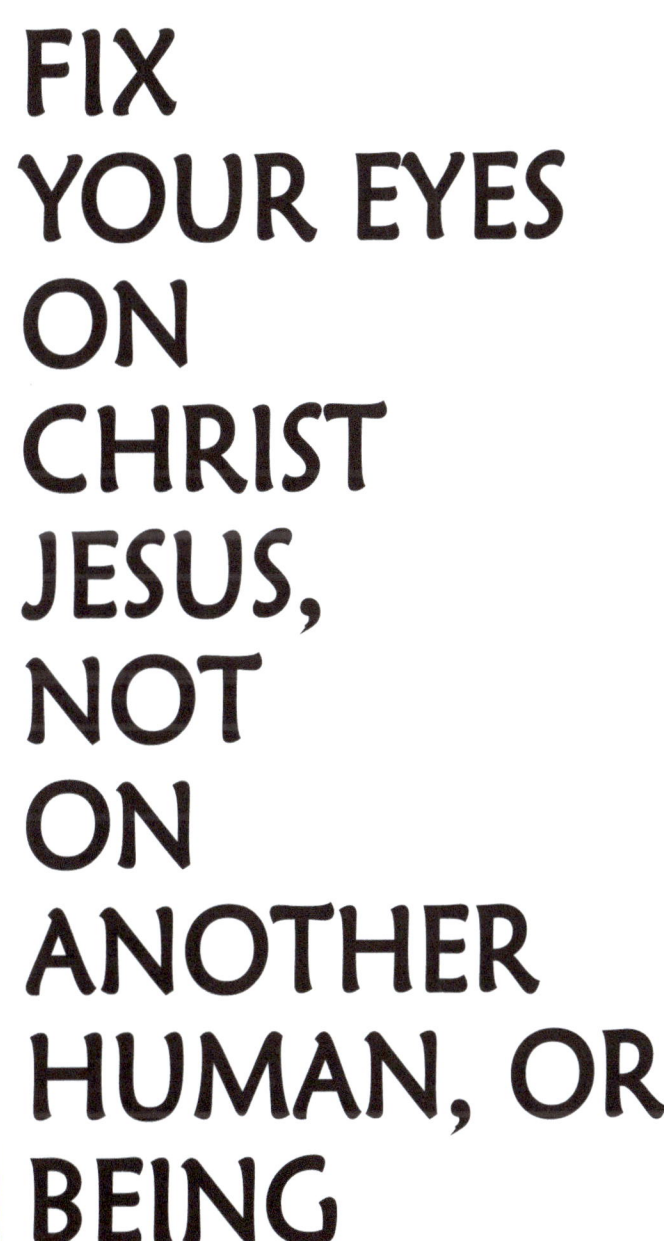

FIX YOUR EYES ON CHRIST JESUS, NOT ON ANOTHER HUMAN, OR BEING

JESUS is LORD GOD ALMIGHTY. Follow him.

Notes

Joshua 1:8
2 Kings 6:15-17
Psalm 23
Isaiah 53:5; 54:17
Ezekiel 2:1-8
John 6:1-59
Romans 12:2
Philippians 4:7-13
James 4:7
1 Peter 1:3-11;
     2:21-24
1 John 4:1-6, 16
3 John 2-11

GREATER IS HE THAT IS IN YOU, THAN he THAT IS IN THE WORLD

JESUS' promised one, the Spirit of truth: John 14:17

Notes

Joy

Genesis 1:1-3
Job 19:25-27
Psalms 16:8-11; 22
Isaiah 53
Daniel 7:13-14, 27
Matthew 9:27-33; 28
Mark 16
Luke 24
John 1:1-5; 20
1 Corinthians 15
1 Peter 3:17-22
Jude 1, 25

HE JOKES IN MATT 9:30; LEAVES A SELFIE IN THE SHROUD OF TURIN: √ JESUS WAS HUMAN, TOO

BE IT DEBTOR OR MOTHER A VOICE GAINS MEANING WITH A FACE

But see that no one knows what you cannot keep to yourself.

Notes

Joy

Nehemiah 3:12
Psalms 23; 100;
     118; 150
Ecclesiastes 3:1-14
Isaiah 42:1-12;
     61:1-3
Matthew 5:1-12
Luke 4:16-22
Romans 8
Galatians 5:22-23
Philippians 3:1-14
1 Thessalonians
     5:14-18
Hebrews 3:13
Jude 24-25

THIS IS THE DAY THAT THE LORD HAS MADE, I WILL REJOICE AND BE GLAD IN IT

AMEN. Ps 118:24

Notes

Joy

1 Kings 17:8-24
2 Kings 4:1-37
Job 19:23-27
Psalms 16:8-11; 22;
    62:11-12
Isaiah 53
Ezekiel 37:1-14
Jonah 1:17
Matthew 9:18-26;
    12:38-41;
    28
Mark 5:21-43; 16
Luke 7:11-17;
    8:40-56;
    11:29-30; 24
John 10:11-33;
    11:1-45; 20
Acts 9:32-43
    20:6-12

WHAT DID THE PREACHER SAY? JESUS HAS RISEN HIMSELF; THE GRAVE COULDN'T HOLD HIM

Grave, where is your victory? 1 Cor 15:55; John 10:17-18

Notes

Psalm 55:12-14
Isaiah 7:15; 53:7
Jeremiah 23:5-6
Daniel 7:13-14, 27
Zechariah 9:9-10;
          12:10
Malachi 3:1-6
Matthew 4:23;
  5; 6; 7; 8:5-13;
  9:35; 10:8;
  14:13-21; 15:32-38;
  26:57-68;
  27:1-31, 57-60
Mark 6:30-44;
  7:24-30; 8:1-9;
  15:1-20
Luke 5:12-15;
  6:1-11, 17-49;
  9:10-17; 23:1-25
John 2:1-11; 3:1-21;
  4:3-42; 6:1-15;
  9:1-41; 11:1-54;
  18:28-40; 19:1-16
Hebrews 13:8
1 Peter 2:21-24

HE SPENT 3 YEARS WITH 5,000+ PEOPLE AND YET HIS WORDS WERE NEVER CONSIDERED A THREAT ... TO ROME JOHN 18:35

JESUS' words? Deut 5; 6:4-9

Notes

Perspective

Gen 3:15; 49:10
Exod 12; 13
Lev 10:1-7; 16
Num 24:17, 19
Deut 18:15-22
2 Sam 7:12-17
Isa 7:14-16; 9:6-7
Jer 23:5-6; 31
Ezek 20:35
Dan 7:27; 9:26
Mic 5:2
John 20:28-29

Regarding JESUS:
- 300+ prophecies between Genesis and Malachi.
- 400+ years of silence between Malachi and Matthew.
- From the OT to the NT, GOD does not change, therefore ...

NUM 24:1-9
PS 22
ISA 53
DAN 7:13-14
ZECH 12:10
MAL 3:1-6
MATT 4:1
MARK 1:12
LUKE 4:1
JOHN 19:34

we are not consumed: Lam 3:21-23; Mal 3:6; John 18:36

Notes

Genesis 1:1-3, 27;
2:4-7
Exodus 3:14; 6:2-3;
15:26
Leviticus 20:7-8;
24:11-21,
(22, 23)
Numbers 6:22-27
Deuteronomy 6:4;
32:3-4
Judges 6:25-26, 31
Job 38
Psalm 107:25-30
Mark 4:35-41
Luke 7:11-15
John 1:1-5; 20:28
2 Thessalonians
2:16-17

WITH EVERY BREATH IN AND OUT OF OUR NOSES, WE SAY THE NAME OF THE GOD OF THE JEWS: YHWH

HE builds upon the rock of our faith: Matt 16:13-18

Notes

Genesis 3:15
Psalms 22; 34:20
Isaiah 50:5-11;
　　　52:14-15; 53
Amos 8:9
Jonah 1:17
Zechariah 12:10
Matthew 12:38-41;
　　　27:45-54
Mark 14:53-65;
　　　15:33-39
Luke 23:44-48
John 10:11-33;
　　　19:30-37

CHRIST JESUS LAID HIS EARTHLY LIFE DOWN. NO ONE TOOK IT FROM HIM

HE is the beginning and the ending: Rev 1:7-8

Notes

Testimony

Genesis 3:15
Psalm 22
Isaiah 52:13-15; 53
Matthew 27; 28
Mark 15; 16
Luke 23; 24
John 18; 19; 20; 21
Exodus 3:13-14
John 8:56-58
Exodus 15:26
Mark 1:21-34
Numbers 24:1
Matthew 4:1
Mark 1:12
Luke 4:1
Daniel 7:13-14, 27
Mark 14:61-62
Pericardial Effusion
John 19:34-37
Josephus
Mara bar Sarapion
Pliny the Younger
Tacitus
Suetonius
Lucian of Samosata

EVIDENCE IN OVER 66 BOOKS. HE DIED, AND WAS BURIED. BUT THEN ... JESUS GOT BACK UP

The Sudarium of Oviedo

The Shroud of Turin Selfie

Tel Dan Stele

Dead Sea Scrolls

MEGIDDO MOSAIC
GAVELLO HEEL BONE
ALEXAMENOS GRAFFITO
PILATE DEDICATION STONE
YEHOHANAN HEEL BONE
CAMBRIDGESHIRE HEEL BONE

... when HE didn't have to: John 10:11-33

Notes

Psalms 16:10; 49:15
John 10:11-33

List of Candidates:
- Alexander the Great? Nope.
- Apollonius of Tyana? Nope.
- Tammuz? Definitey not.
- Jesus? Bingo.

Testimony

HE WAS BORN OF A VIRGIN, DIED, WAS BURIED, AND ROSE FROM THE GRAVE ON THE THIRD DAY

And, HE died for our sins: 1 Cor 15:3-11

Notes

Trust GOD

Genesis 4:1
Exodus 32:7-35;
        33:1-17
Deuteronomy 31:8
Joshua 1:5
2 Chronicles 15:2
Isaiah 41:9-17;
        54:10
Jeremiah 1:8
Matthew 28:18-20
John 13:36-38;
        18:1-27; 21
1 Timothy 1:12-17
2 Timothy 3:10-11;
        4:1-8
Hebrews 13:5

HINDSIGHT REVEALS JESUS WILL NEVER LEAVE YOU, NOR WILL HE EVER FORSAKE YOU

Keep the faith.

Notes

Trust GOD

Psalms 18:1-3; 23;
27;
34:13-19; 62
Proverbs 3:5-6
Isaiah 41:10-13;
52:7
Nahum 1:7
Matthew 18:15-35
Luke 17:1-4
Romans 8:24-28
1 Corinthians 2:1-5
Ephesians 4:1-2
Philippians 1:27-28
1 Peter 2:12
Jude 3

... IT'S YOUR PRESENCE IN THAT PLACE THAT GOD REQUIRES — BECAUSE OF YOUR FAITH 1 THESS 5:14-24

Keep JESUS' words in you, and the devil will flee.

Notes

Trust GOD

NO MATTER WHERE WE GO, THERE WILL NEVER BE A PLACE WHERE I AM IS NOT

Genesis 3:8-24;
4:1
Exodus 3:14-15;
14:21-30
Job 26:6-14
Psalms 23; 139:7-10
Song of Solomon
8:13
Isaiah 45:5-6
Daniel 7:13-14, 27
Jonah 1:17; 2:1-10
Matthew 10:29-31;
14:22-33
Mark 6:45-51;
14:61-62
Luke 12:6-7
John 8:56-58;
20:28-29

JUDG 13 - 16
1 SAM 5:1-5
2 KGS 6:15-17
ACTS 9:1-19

CONTEND
FOR THE FAITH
ONCE
DELIVERED
TO US ALL
TRUST GOD

Walk where I AM shines HIS light: Ps 119:105-112

Notes

Trust in GOD

Ruth 1:1-16, 4:13-22
2 Samuel 12:1-25
Esther 4:10 - 7:10
Psalms 20; 23; 27
Daniel 3; 6
Habakkuk 3:17-19
Zephaniah 3:12-20
Zechariah 4:6-10
Luke 18:1-8
John 4:1-42
1 Timothy 1:12-17
Philemon 8-21

AS THE WIND CHANGES, SO TOO CAN OUR SITUATIONS; THEREFORE, TRUST IN THE LORD

GOD will never leave you, so don't you leave GOD.

Notes

Trust in GOD

Psalms 20; 23; 91
Proverbs 3:5-6
Micah 6:8
Matthew 17:14-21;
        21:18-22
Mark 9:14-27
Luke 1:37
John 14:1-9; 20:29
Romans 1:17;
        8:35-39
2 Corinthians 5:6-9
Colossians 2:6-10
2 Timothy 1:7-12;
        4:5-7
Hebrews 11

PUT YOUR TRUST IN JESUS AND YOU WILL WALK BY FAITH, AND NOT BY SIGHT HOS 14:9

JESUS knows and is the way. Follow HIM.

Notes

Psalm 1
Psalm 27
Psalm 34
Psalm 115
Psalm 10
Psalm 35
Psalm 94
Psalm 143
Psalm 4
Psalm 91
Psalm 103
Psalm 125

WHEN IT BECOMES TOO MUCH, (PSALM 88) HOLD TIGHT TO YOUR TRUST IN GOD. PSALM 61 PSALM 23 HE WILL SEE YOU THRU

From faith thru anger to trust, hold on to GOD: Ps 20

Notes

Belief

Genesis 1:1 - 2:2;
49:8-12
Exodus 3:13-15;
15:26;
25:17-22
Leviticus 10:1-7;
16:1-34
Numbers 7:89;
24:1-9,
17-19
Deuteronomy 6:4;
18:15-22;
32:39
Psalms 22; 95:6-8
Isaiah 7:14; 53
Malachi 3:1-6; 4
Matthew 1:18-23
Mark 1:21-27
Luke 1:17, 26-45;
2:21
John 1:1-5; 2:18-19;
10:27-33;
14:8-11;
19:34;
20:26-29

WHO DO YOU SAY JESUS IS?

DAN 7:13-14, 27
ZECH 12:10

GOD ALMIGHTY, WRAPPED IN FLESH

Emmanuel, the Mercy Seat of GOD.

Notes

Faith

Job 42:1-6
Psalms 25; 31; 139
Isaiah 40:8-9; 52:7
Hosea 1:1-2;
        5:13 - 6:6;
        10:12; 14:9
Joel 2:12-13
Nahum 1:3, 7
Matthew 6:5-15;
        26:33-35,
        47-75
Luke 18:9-14
John 13:36-38;
        18:1-27; 21
Romans 10:8-15
1 Thessalonians
    5:14-18
2 Peter 3:9-18

SHAME CAN PREVENT PRAYER

PRAYER

CHANGES THINGS

THINGS

THAT ONLY GOD CAN SEE

In every situation, pray without ceasing. 1 Sam 1:6-20

Notes

Forgiveness

Exodus 34:6-7
Leviticus 19:17-18
Psalms 32; 86
Proverbs 19:11
Lamentations
  3:21-23
Micah 6:8; 7:18
Matthew 6:14-15;
  18:15-35
Mark 11:25-26
Luke 6:27-28;
  17:3-10
John 13:34-35;
  15:12-13
Ephesians 4:32
Jude 3

AGAINST THIS, THE DEVIL HAS NO WEAPON: FORGIVE YOURSELF FORGIVE OTHERS FORGIVE ME

Contend for the faith once delivered to us: Forgive.

Notes

Identity

Genesis 1:1-3,
26-28;
3:15; 15:1;
49:10
Exodus 15:2
Numbers 6:22-27;
24:1-9,
17, 19
Deuteronomy
33:29
2 Samuel 22:3,
31-36
Psalms 3:3; 18:1-2;
20; 28:7;
33:20;
115:9; 121
Proverbs 30:5
Isaiah 43:1; 52:12
John 1:1-5, 11-13
Romans 8:1-2, 16
2 Corinthians 5:17
Ephesians 1:5; 6:16

HE IS THE MAGEN, SHIELD, OF DAVID AND IN HIM I FIND MY IDENTITY: HE IS JESUS

THE LIVING GOD

DEUT 5:26
1 SAM 17:26

Trust in him, JESUS: the Shield of David, HASHEM.

Notes

Integrity

1 Chronicles
  16:11-12
Proverbs 24:16-20
Isaiah 43:1-2
Jeremiah 29:11-13
Micah 7:7-10, 18
Haggai 1:5-14
John 13:36-38;
        18:1-27; 21
Romans 8:28
2 Corinthians 4:6-9
Philippians 1:6,
          12-18
James 1:2-8
2 John 4-11

AS A CHILD YOU FELL MANY TIMES BEFORE YOU LEARNED TO WALK: CHILD OF GOD, GET BACK UP

Remember who GOD is, and get back up.

Notes

Gen 2:2; 3:15; 22
Exod 6:1; 20:1-17;
   23:30;
   25:17-22;
   33:2;
   34:11-13, 24
Deut 5:26; 7:1-5,
   16-26; 9:3-5;
   11:22-23;
   29:1-6; 32:35
Judg 2:1-3, 19-23;
   3:1-4
1 Samuel 10:8;
   11:1-3; 13:8-14;
   14:37; 15:1-3,
   20-22, 30; 17:26
Isa 6:8-10; 55:6-11
Jer 5:21; 7:22-23;
   32:17
Ezek 8; 12:2
Hos 4:1-6; 6:4-6
Zech 4:6
Mal 3:6
Matt 4:1-11;
   9:9 - 12:13;
   13:9-16;
   22:34-40

FROM THE RISING OF THE SUN UNTIL THE GOING DOWN OF THE SAME, GOD DOES NOT CHANGE

PS 113:3

PS 111:10
PROV 9:10

LEV 24:10-21, (22-23)
NUM 15:27-34, (35-36)
LUKE 7:11-16

2 KGS 6:15-17
ROM 12:18-21

... WE DO

Wait on the LORD: Prov 20:22. Matt 9:13

Notes

Love

Leviticus 19:9-18
Deuteronomy
  32:35
Proverbs 16:6;
     25:21-22
Amos 5:21-24
Obadiah 15-17
Jonah 3:1 - 4:11
Malachi 3:1-6
Matthew 7:1-12
Mark 12:28-34
Luke 6:27-38
Romans 12:1-21
1 John 4:4, 18-21

DO UNTO OTHERS AS YOU WOULD HAVE THEM DO UNTO YOU

For this is the law and the prophets: Matt 7:12

Notes

Peace

Numbers 6:22-27
Psalms 19:14; 23;
        27; 34;
        37; 91;
        119:105-112
Isaiah 26:1-4
Matthew 4:1-11;
        5:1-16;
        6:8-15
Luke 4:1-13;
      4:6:17-23;
      11:1-4
Romans 12:2; 14
1 Corinthians
  12:1-14
2 Corinthians
  10:3-5
Galatians 5:22-26
Philippians 4:8, 13
Colossians 3:1-2, 8
1 Thessalonians
  5:14-18

IN JESUS' NAME, WHATEVER IS GOOD WHATEVER IS LOVING, THINK ON THESE THINGS

DEUT 8:3

DEUT 6:16

DEUT 6:13, 10:20

ALWAYS REPLACE EVIL THOUGHTS WITH SCRIPTURE

... and the devil will flee.

Notes

Revelation

Genesis 12:5; 16:1;
23:1;
24:15;
25:1;
29; 30; 38
Exodus 1:15; 2:1-21;
6:20-25;
15:20
Leviticus 24:11
Numbers 26:33,
46;
27:1-11
Joshua 2; 6:17-25
Judges 4; 5; 11:34
1 Samuel 1:1-28
2 Kings 22:11-20;
2 Chronicles
34:19-28
Nehemiah 3:12
Luke 1:13-31;
2:36-37;
7:11-15
Acts 18:2, 26;
21:8-9

SOMETHING TO THINK ABOUT: MATT 14:21 BESIDE 5,000 MEN. ADD IN THE WOMEN, RUTH ESTHER ROM 16 AND IT'S AN ARMY ...

how beautiful their feet. Isa 52:7; Nah 1:15; Rom 10:15

Notes

Self-Control

Judges 11:30-31, 34
Psalms 103:8; 145:8
Proverbs 10:19;
14:29;
15:1-4;
16:32;
18:21;
25:21-22
Ecclesiastes 7:9
Matthew 5:38-48
Mark 3:1-6
Luke 6:26-36
John 15:12
Acts 10; 11:1-18
Romans 12:14-21
Ephesians 4:26-32
James 1:19-20

BE SLOW TO ANGER, AND SLOWER TO SPEAK SO THAT YOU SIN NOT

Looks can be deceiving. Hold your peace: Exod 14:14

Notes

Self-Worth

Genesis 1:27-28;
4:1
1 Samuel 1:1-28
1 Chronicles 16:11
Psalms 20; 23; 27;
139
Isaiah 26:3-4;
31:1-3
Jeremiah 1:5;
29:1-11
Matthew 10:29-31;
18:10-14
Luke 10:38-42;
12:6-7; 15:4-7
John 3:16; 8:1-12
Romans 5:6-8
Titus 3:1-5; 4:1-5
Hebrews 11

FIND YOUR SELF-WORTH IN JESUS: HE LEFT THE 99 JUST TO FIND YOU HIMSELF

NEVER FORGET

You're just that important to GOD.

Notes

The Truth

Genesis 1:1-3; 3:15
Deuteronomy 6:4
John 1:1-5; 14:5-9
Isaiah 7:14-16
Luke 1:17, 24-35; 2:21
Jonah 1:17
Matthew 12:38-42
Leviticus 19:18;
Matthew 19:16-26
Luke 10:25-37
Leviticus 24:10-21
Luke 7:11-16
2 Kings 6:15-23
Matthew 26:46-56
Mark 14:42-52
Luke 22:46-53
John 18:3-12
Exodus 14:13-31
Isaiah 43:2
Matthew 8:23-27; 14:22-33
Mark 6:45-51
Luke 8:22-25
John 6:15-21

THEY SAY JESUS WAS JUST A GOOD MAN. BUT, HOW DO THEY KNOW THAT?

HE NEVER DID A MIRACLE FOR SHOW, OR EVEN TO SAVE HIMSELF. SO

JOHN 5:46

DEUT 18:15-22
MARK 2:1-12

EXOD 15:26
MARK 1:21-28

HE was more than that: John 20:24-29

65

Notes

Pastors of God:

תודה *Mvto*

Nitsiniiyi'taki

ありがとう Asante شكرًا لك GV આભાર Mulțumesc

Takk Ευχαριστώ Ahíyi'é ขอบคุณ Tack

Medaase

Merci Askwali Teşekkür ederim *Gracias*

Kwaʹkwah Děkuji Ďakujem Tak

Galatoomi Dank je wel

Mahalo Hvala Ahéhee' Daalų

Спасибо *in Jesus' name* Mèsi Ačiū

E dupe شكريه Pilamaya 谢谢 धन्यवाद

Sho-No-Bish ధన్యవాదాలు Na gode Ngā mihi

ਧੰਨਵਾਦ *Obrigada* Dziękuję धन्यवाद

Obrigado Enkosi Natotela Hahom

감사합니다 Дякую متشكرم Cảm ơn

Danke Hatur nuhun *Niá:wen* Благодарам

Grazie Köszönöm Aishen Terima kasih

நன்றி Благодаря *thank you!*

 አመሰግናለሁ Salamat

Tatenda Jërëjëf *You are appreciated!*

Ngiyabonga

Thank You in 84 Languages (Only because that's all that would fit on this page.)

1 አመሰግናለሁ (Amharic - Ethiopia {Ameseginalew})
2 شكرا لك (Arabic {Shukran Lak})
3 ধন্যবাদ (Bengali {Dhonyobaad})
4 Благодаря (Bulgarian {Blagodarya})
5 ᎠᎣᎥ (Cherokee (Tsalagi) - U.S. {Wah-doe})
6 Ευχαριστώ (Greek {Efcharistó})
7 આભાર (Gujarati - India {Ābhāra})
8 תודה (Hebrew {Toda})
9 धन्यवाद (Hindi - India {Dhanyavaad})
10 ありがとう (Japanese {Arigatou})
11 감사합니다 (Korean {Gamsahabnida})
12 Благодарам (Macedonian {Blagodaram})
13 متشکرم (Persian {Moteshkaram})
14 ਧੰਨਵਾਦ (Punjabi - India {Dhanvaad})
15 Спасибо (Russian {Spasibo})
16 Хвала (Serbian)*
17 நன்றி (Tamil - India {Nandri})
18 ధన్యవాదాలు (Telugu - India {Dhan'yavādālu})
19 ขอบคุณ (Thai {Khob khun})
20 谢谢 (Mandarin Chinese {Xièxiè})
21 Дякую (Ukrainian {Dyakuyu})
22 شکریہ (Urdu - Pakistan {Shukriya})
23 Ačiū (Lithuanian)
24 Ahéhee' (Navajo (Diné Bizaad) - U.S.)
25 Ahíyi'é (Bylas Apache - U.S.)
26 Aishen (Shoshone - Idaho, U.S.)
27 Aitäh (Estonian)*
28 Asante (Kiswahili)
29 Askwali (used by women) / Kwa'kwah (used by men) (Hopi - U.S.)
30 Cảm ơn (Vietnamese)
31 Daalụ (Igbo - Nigeria)
32 Ďakujem (Slovak)
33 Dank je wel (Dutch)
34 Danke (German)
35 Dankie (Afrikaans - South Africa)*
36 Děkuji (Czech)
37 Dziękuję (Polish)
38 E dupe (Yoruba - Nigeria)
39 Elahkwa (Zuni - U.S.)*
40 Enkosi (Xhosa - South Africa)
41 Faleminderit (Albanian)*
42 Galatoomi (singular) / Galatoomaa (plural) (Oromo - Ethiopia; Kenya)

43 Gracias (Spanish)
44 Grazie (Italian)
45 Gunalchéesh (Tlingit - Alaska, U.S.)*
46 Hahom (Taino - Caribbean)
47 Hatur nuhun (Sundanese - Sudan)
48 Hvala (Bosnian; Croatian; Slovenian)
49 Jërëjëf (Wolof - Senegal; Gambia; Mauritania)
50 Káwruwa (Pawnee - U.S.)*
51 Ke a leboga (Setswana - Botswana; South Africa)*
52 Kea leboha (Sesotho - Lesotho; South Africa; Zimbabwe)*
53 Köszönöm (Hungarian)
54 Kutâputush (Wampanoag - U.S.)*
55 Mahadsanid (Somali - Somalia)*
56 Mahalo (Hawaiian - U.S.)
57 Medaase (Twi - Ghana)
58 Merci (French)
59 Mèsi (Haitian Creole)
60 Miigwech (Ojibwe (Anishinaabemowin) - U.S.)*
61 Mulțumesc (Romanian)
62 Murakoze (Kinyarwanda - Rwanda)*
63 Mvto (Creek (Mvskoke) - U.S. {Muhdoe})
64 Na gode (Hausa - Nigeria; Niger)
65 Natotela (Bemba - Zambia)
66 Ngā mihi (Māori - New Zealand)
67 Ngiyabonga (singular) / Siyabonga (plural) (Zulu - Lesotho; South Africa)
68 Nia:wen (Mohawk (Kanyen'kehá) - U.S.)
69 Nitsiniiyi'taki (Blackfoot (Siksiká) - U.S.)
70 Obrigado (used by men) / Obrigada (used by women) (Portuguese)
71 Paldies (Latvian)*
72 Pilamaya (Lakota Sioux - U.S.)
73 Qujannamiik (Inuit (Inuktut) - Alaska, U.S.; Canada)*
74 Salamat (Filipino (Tagalog) - Philippines)
75 Sho-Na-Bish (Seminole - U.S.)
76 Tack (Swedish)
77 Tak (Danish)
78 Takk (Icelandic; Norwegian)
79 Tatenda (Shona - Zimbabwe)
80 Terima kasih (Indonesian; Malay)
81 Teşekkür ederim (Turkish)
82 Weebale (Luganda - Uganda)*
83 Yakoke (Choctaw/Chickasaw - U.S. {Yahkohke})*
84 Zikomo (Chichewa - Malawi)*

Layout Key: Thank You (Group (Language) / Language - Country {Pronunciation})
*No space to place these on my "You are appreciated!" illustration.
Note: "U.S." means the United States of America.

Notes

Psalm 23 (KJV; bold/italic emphasis mine, comma added in verse 5 between "me" and "in," and colon removed from between "enemies," and "thou")
1 The Lord is my shepherd; I shall not want.
2 He maketh me to lie down in green pastures: he leadeth me beside the still waters.
3 He restoreth my soul: he leadeth me in the paths of righteousness for his name's sake.
4 Yea, though I walk *through* the valley of the shadow of death, I will fear no evil: for thou art with me; thy rod and thy staff they comfort me.
5 Thou preparest a table before me[,] *in the presence of mine enemies thou anointest my head with oil*; my cup runneth over.
6 Surely goodness and mercy shall follow me all the days of my life: and I will dwell in the house of the Lord for ever.

Bible Study Tips
During your study, have at least three or more translations of the Bible on hand so that you can compare different translations. When you notice major differences in translations, it means that the original text (Hebrew or Greek) could not easily be translated into English without disturbing the word order of the original. To fully understand such verses when you come upon them, it is best to consult the original text.

Here are a few resources for doing that:
- biblegateway.com
- biblehub.com
- blueletterbible.org
- logos.com
- biblestudytools.com
- gotquestions.org

Here are some other useful resources:
- chabad.org
- myjewishlearning.com
- oneforisrael.org
- biblicalarchaeology.org

One Bible that I recommend that you get for your library is the "KJV Personal Size Giant Print Reference Bible" ISBN: 9781598562460, published by Hendrickson. I love this KJV Bible because the publisher provides in-line cross-references.

Other versions that I recommend include the following. With all of these versions, try to get hardcopy and ebook "Study Bible" editions.
- Holman Christian Standard Bible (HCSB)
- Mounce Reverse Interlinear New Testament (MRINT)
- New American Standard Bible (NASB)
- New International Version (NIV)
- New Revised Standard Version Updated Edition (get the NRSV with the Apocrypha edition)

Here are a few good books to have in your library to help with your study of the Bible:
- How to Choose a Translation for All Its Worth by Gordon D. Fee and Mark L. Strauss, ISBN 9780310278764
- The New Testament Canon: Its Making and Meaning, A Guide to Biblical Scholarship by Harry Y. Gamble, ISBN 9781579109097
- Synopsis of the Four Gospels, Revised Standard Version, Edited by Kurt Aland, ISBN 9781585169429 (Out of print, but great resource if you can find a used or new one reasonably priced. I paid the reasonable price of $37.47 USD for a new one in December 2023. I recently saw one selling online for about $125.00 USD.)
- Rose Book of Bible Charts, Maps & Time Lines, ISBN 9781596360228

I recommend the following authors be added to your library solely for the sake of understanding arguments for and against Christianity. I do not agree with everything in their scholarship, and I have my reasons as to why. The challenge for you is to understand your own reasons for and against their scholarship. In other words, when the time comes, what will be your own reason for believing in CHRIST JESUS, the living GOD? What will be your 1 Peter 3:13-15 response?
- The following author I recommend for those seeking to understand atheist arguments against the Christian faith. One book of his that I recommend, "The New Testament: A Historical Introduction to the Early Christian Writings," sixth edition by Bart D. Ehrman, ISBN 978-0190203825, details the history of Christianity. Bart is a well-respected historian who calls himself a Christian atheist. The current eighth edition, ISBN 978-0197754023, includes the authorship of Hugo Méndez. Bart's approach is fair-minded, and based on historical evidence rather than appeals to emotion. His Web address is bartehrman.com.
- Nabeel Qureshi's book, "Seeking Allah, Finding Jesus: A Devout Muslim Encounters Christianity" ISBN 978-0310092643, I recommend because he was someone who sought the truth, and not tradition or emotion. Although Nabeel was taken home to be with the LORD on September 16, 2017, you can hear his testimony on YouTube at this link as well as on other YouTube channels: Muslim converts to Christianity after realising the Bible is true // The Profile. His Website is maintained at nabeelqureshi.com.

Key to Abbreviations

Note: The Christian OT was developed from the Jewish Tanakh (the Hebrew Bible). TaNaKh is an acronym for Torah (Instruction/Law/Pentateuch), Nevi'im (Prophets), and Ketuvim (Writings). The Tanakh's divisions were reordered in the Christian Bible from Torah, Prophets, and Writings to Torah, Historical Writings, Wisdom Writings, and Prophets because that order looked forward to the prophesied Christ, our (Jewish) Messiah.

Old Testament (OT)
1. Genesis (Gen)
2. Exodus (Exod)
3. Leviticus (Lev)
4. Numbers (Num)
5. Deuteronomy (Deut)
6. Joshua (Josh)
7. Judges (Judg)
8. Ruth (Ruth)
9. 1 Samuel (1 Sam)
10. 2 Samuel (2 Sam)
11. 1 Kings (1Kgs)
12. 2 Kings (2Kgs)
13. 1 Chronicles (1 Chr)
14. 2 Chronicles (2 Chr)
15. Ezra (Ezra)
16. Nehemiah (Neh)
17. Esther (Esth)
18. Job (Job)
19. Psalms (Ps, plural Pss)
20. Proverbs (Prov)
21. Ecclesiastes (Eccl)
22. Song of Solomon (Song)
23. Isaiah (Isa)
24. Jeremiah (Jer)
25. Lamentations (Lam)
26. Ezekiel (Ezek)
27. Daniel (Dan)
28. Hosea (Hos)
29. Joel (Joel)
30. Amos (Amos)
31. Obadiah (Obad)
32. Jonah (Jonah)
33. Micah (Mic)
34. Nahum (Nah)
35. Habakkuk (Hab)
36. Zephaniah (Zeph)
37. Haggai (Hag)
38. Zechariah (Zech)
39. Malachi (Mal)

New Testament (NT)
1. Matthew (Matt)
2. Mark (Mark)
3. Luke (Luke)
4. John (John)
5. Acts (Acts)
6. Romans (Rom)
7. 1 Corinthians (1 Cor)
8. 2 Corinthians (2 Cor)
9. Galatians (Gal)
10. Ephesians (Eph)
11. Philippians (Phil)
12. Colossians (Col)
13. 1 Thessalonians (1 Thess)
14. 2 Thessalonians (2 Thess)
15. 1 Timothy (1 Tim)
16. 2 Timothy (2 Tim)
17. Titus (Titus)
18. Philemon (Phlm)
19. Hebrews (Heb)
20. James (Jas)
21. 1 Peter (1 Pet)
22. 2 Peter (2 Pet)
23. 1 John (1 John)
24. 2 John (2 John)
25. 3 John (3 John)
26. Jude (Jude)
27. Revelation (Rev)